Note from the author

GW00857350

I am a CIMA MiP and a business ow

Having qualified in 1993 I have sin
range of businesses, from multinationals to small ...
managed businesses.

As a MiP I have built my business by providing management accountancy services to small and medium sized businesses in deepest Somerset.

Over the years I have found that MiPs often don't have the businesses they want, not because they are not capable of doing so, but because they make assumptions that are just not helpful. This handbook is designed to show how a successful management accounting businesses can be built.

None of what I will talk about is rocket science, and other MiPs may have different experiences, but after 15 years in practice, 10 of which running my own business, I have plenty of experience to share.

As you will only make real changes to your business by committing to that change, at the end of each chapter you will find; an exercise so you can relate what you have read to your own business; a place to note what specifically you have learned from the chapter; and a place to commit to changing your behaviour in the future.

Copyright © 2017 Bevan Financial Management Ltd.
All rights reserved. No part of this publication may be reproduced without prior permission of the author.

Section	Contents	Page
Section	**Contents**	**Page**

SECTION 1

Introduction

Introduction

There are two basic models of MiP business based on having multiple clients (as opposed to interims). Some MiPs will be tax and compliance specialists, and some will be purely management accounting specialists or consultants. Still others will be a mixture of the two.

The way in which you market your business will depend upon which model you would like to follow, so it is important that you decide as soon as you can which model your business should be based upon.

Whichever model you choose should be founded on your skills and experience.

If you are not a tax and compliance expert – ideally with tax qualifications under your belt – you should not be selling your services as a tax and compliance accountant.

If you have not worked at managerial/board level in a variety of businesses, you will not have the broad experience needed to act as a part time FD/management accountant for clients – unless you can niche in an area you have got experience in.

Our clients deserve the best. If we are the best at providing a particular service - happy days! If we are not, we should leave it to other professionals who are.

Key features of the different business models for CIMA MiPs:

Compliance and tax (excludes detailed tax planning services):

Average annual client-facing days per client - 1-2

Average annual fee income per client - £500-£5000

Average number of clients per professional - 200-300

Average time taken to sign a new client from standing start - 1-6 months

[Because the compliance and tax work is readily understood by the market it is relatively easy to start getting clients].

Management accounting/part time FD:

Average annual client- facing days per client - 12-50

Average annual fee income per client - £7000-£30000

Average number of clients per professional - 5-10

Average time taken to sign a new client from a standing start - 6 months +

[It takes longer to start signing up management accounting clients because SME owners do not know what we do and doing management accounting work is generally more labour intensive leading to fairly large ticket prices]

Are you suited to offering management accounting (in its broader concept)?

Do you like working with people more than figures?

If you wish to offer more management accounting than compliance services you will need to spend quite a lot of time, on a regular basis, working in your clients' businesses. If you would prefer to be working on your own perhaps this route is not for you.

Have you experience of different businesses and sectors?

To be effective as a business advisor you need to be experienced in a number of different business types and sectors. If your experience is limited to one business and/or sector you will struggle to be able to offer robust guidance to businesses in other sectors. However, this does not mean that you could not set up your business advising businesses in the sector you <u>are</u> familiar with.

Do you like to be doing something different every day?

As a management accounting based MiP there are no 'same days'. With compliance work you may well be doing the same work for all your clients but with management accounting each client will be different and will have different demands on your time.

Are you passionate about solving problems?

We will often be the only business advisor working for a client. This means that we are called upon to help solve problems with the business owner – some of which will be outside the normal scope of accountancy.

If you are intimidated by the prospect of having to offer quick and efficient problem solving you will struggle to give the type of support clients need.

Are you happy to meet new people and find out what makes them tick?

If you want to be effective you will need to be able to quickly work out what is going on within a business and this will mean working out what's going on with the business owner.

You will need to be prepared to ask challenging questions of your clients, so you can best help them move their business forward.

EXERCISE

Answer each of the questions above honestly.

If you have answered NO to any of them you may find you are not suited to running a management accounting business. If you answered YES to them all read on.

Learning and action steps

Don't forget to fill this section - it can make a real difference to how much you learn from the handbook and how useful it is in helping you build the business you want.

<u>Actions I will start doing</u>   <u>Importance</u>   <u>Date</u>

<u>Actions I will stop doing</u>   <u>Importance</u>   Date

taking on'tg time
bkkpg accnts

Behaviour change log

Today's date _____

Review Date   Reviewed   Outstanding Issues

Tomorrow

1 week

1 month

3 months

SECTION 2

What is management accounting in the SME context?

What SMEs need

Management accounting is so much more than providing monthly or quarterly management accounts -which is just as well, given that even the most basic accounting package can provide a profit and loss and balance sheet.

Being a management accountant for SMEs is much more like being a part time Financial Director. Our role is to provide help and guidance across all the financial areas of the business.

Terminology

I see the terms 'management accountant', 'virtual FD' and 'part time FD' as indistinguishable from each other when applied to the SME market. So in the rest of this book I will be using the terms interchangeably.

A sounding board

Because we may be the only outside advisor the business owner has with whom to bounce around ideas, we are often involved in areas of the business decision making process not traditionally seen as within the accounting sphere.

We can find ourselves involved in discussions around the employment of new staff; marketing planning; staff training, IT issues etc.

Many business owners are stopped from moving their businesses forward because they just cannot make a decision - usually because they don't feel they have enough information to make the right one. Instead they come to a stalemate situation, which is actually worse than making a decision - even if it is not the 'best' one.

So, our role is to provide information and support to allow the business owner/s to make strong strategic decisions.

Business planning

As we know business planning is the best tool we have available to assist in the formulation of strategy.

Assisting business owners in drawing up business plans, so they explore all aspects of their business and the role these aspects play in the success, or otherwise, is another key role for us.

A business plan can force them to look under the bonnet of their business to find out what really makes it tick. Once they have done that we can help them put numbers to the many facets of their company. Our knowledge of KPIs, and other management accounting tools, can help our clients properly understand what drives their business – and so what they need to concentrate on.

Regular management information

A large part of the job is forecasting KPIs, profit and cash flow on a what/if basis so different scenarios can be played through and the best course decided upon.

Then, of course, it is measuring what actually happens against the plan. Having real time, regularly updated year end predictions helps our clients to make decisive moves forwards.

A guide to best practice

Business owners are generally very focused on 'getting the job done' – producing whatever the products or services their business provides - but are often not very knowledgeable when it comes to the best practice 'management' of the business.

We can help our clients to adopt best practice from our extensive experience of how good businesses operate.

So, I like to look at our role as being decision facilitators and part time FDs rather than 'management accountants' - this is great, because that is exactly the role our CIMA qualification best prepares us for!

EXERCISE

Refresh your knowledge of business planning techniques if you have not used them for a while and investigate what tools you may need to do robust and comprehensive forecasting and budgeting with clients.

Learning and action steps

Don't forget to fill this section – it can make a real difference to how much you learn from the handbook and how useful it is in helping you build the business you want.

Actions I will start doing   Importance   Date

Actions I will stop doing   Importance   Date

Behaviour change log

Today's date _____

<table>
<tr><td>__Review Date__</td><td>__Reviewed__</td><td>__Outstanding Issues__</td></tr>
<tr><td>Tomorrow</td><td></td><td></td></tr>
<tr><td>1 week</td><td></td><td></td></tr>
<tr><td>1 month</td><td></td><td></td></tr>
<tr><td>3 months</td><td></td><td></td></tr>
</table>

SECTION 3

IDENTIFYING CUSTOMERS

Is all the world our stage?

Our key problem in engaging customers is not that we are competition for each other (or that traditional accountants do what we do) but that there is not enough recognition in the market place of what we do.

Most SME owners do not have the vaguest idea what value we can bring to their business. They don't know what management accountants do, or if they do, don't understand the benefit we can specifically bring to *their* business.

Another problem we have is that when someone in business refers to 'accountants' the image in every SME's mind is of someone who prepares tax returns and does compliance. If you want to concentrate on management accounting rather than tax and compliance, you can find yourself engaged in conversations about what you don't' do rather than what you do do- something to be avoided.

There are two key ways MiPs who want to focus on virtual FD work can do to help customers to find them. Firstly, correctly identify the size of business that will want, and need, what we do and secondly niche the services offered.

Optimal client size

With regard to the first point, many MiPs will assume that any SME business will need and want what they do. Whilst there is no doubting that all SMEs *need* what we can provide, only a few will *want* it - either because they cannot afford it or because the business owners do not value it.

All businesses require someone to do the statutory accounts and tax and any business we provide regular services for will need to have an effective bookkeeping function (we certainly don't want to be doing bookkeeping). So if a prospect can only afford these two functions they will not be able to afford us!

Good prospects for us will also need to be of a size where the business owners no longer feel capable of running the finance function themselves.

In general, businesses with a minimum turnover of £500k (for service companies) and £1m for companies selling products are of the right size for us. The upper limit is around £10m, because by this stage the business will require a full time Financial Controller/FD.

Incidentally, do not make the mistake of thinking that you can offer bookkeeping services to a client and then move them up to management accounting. If you are charging them the usual bookkeeping rate of £25-£30 per hour, why would they spend £75 per hour with you for strategic management accounting? To them there is not much difference and you have proved your worth is only £25-30 per hour. You are better than bookkeeping - believe it and the right clients will believe it too.

Also, just because you have compliance and tax clients, who pay you £75 per hour for those services, does not mean that they are ready, or able, to spend further cash on management accounting services. They have to pay for tax and compliance to meet their legal requirements, but if they don't believe more regular financial information is beneficial, they won't be prepared to pay for the additional services. Or, they may value the additional services but not yet have the resources to pay for it (if this is the case it is worth nurturing them so when they are able to pay, they know you are able to provide the services they want).

Niching

Niching is very important in helping you get in front of the right clients. You can either niche by offering services to a particular industry, or by being niche in the services you offer.

In the first instance you may have particular interest or experience in an industry you have worked in previously - even if that experience was gained whilst you were an employee.

If you have such experience you can be invaluable to an SME in that sector. You will have insights into the specific problems generated by operating in that sector and may well give them access to solutions they would never have come to on their own.

Prospects will also recognise that your experience is more relevant to them than an accountant who has never worked within their industry. You can talk their talk and walk their walk. Do not underestimate how important that can be in winning work.

Alternatively, you can present yourself as a particular expert in the type of work you do. I am very clear that I am expert at helping businesses owners to master their finances. I provide management information to help them run their business and make the right decisions for them.

I am not expert at tax; compliance; or the intricacies of VAT. I don't do bookkeeping; sales and marketing; HR consultancy or payroll. My clients deserve the best and I am the best at providing a specific set of services Work I am not the best at, I leave to others who are.

Because I am very clear on what I do, referrers are similarly clear and I get the right types of referrals for my business.

Building a Team

It is worth saying here that just because I don't do everything a client needs does not mean that I leave them in the lurch. I have a team of professionals, who are expert in their fields, whom I can call on to fill the gaps. These professionals are essential to my business as they help my clients to have the best help and advice possible.

So if you are niching on services as a virtual FD you will need to have these other professionals on hand to recommend to clients:

- tax and compliance accountants (if you are not completely competent to do yourself)
- bookkeepers
- VAT experts
- payroll and pension service providers
- HR advisors
- sales and marketing strategists
- finance providers and brokers
- software systems providers

It is good to remember that there will be times when you will meet potential clients who are just not right for you. Either you don't provide the services they want or the client is too small. In these cases refer them straight onto someone else. You will be doing the right thing for the customer and the person you refer them to will be grateful too.

EXERCISE

Think through your career so far and list your particular specialisms either in terms of tasks or business sectors.

If you already have clients review whether any of them are of the right size to offer management accounting services and draw up a short list of ones you will target.

Learning and action steps

Don't forget to fill this section – it can make a real difference to how much you learn from the handbook and how useful it is in helping you build the business you want.

Actions I will start doing   Importance   Date

Actions I will stop doing   Importance   Date

Behaviour change log

Today's date _____

Review Date	Reviewed	Outstanding Issues
Tomorrow		
1 week		
1 month		
3 months		

SECTION 4

Choosing Key Partners

Who should be in our team?

As I said in the previous chapter, if you are intending to niche your business to cover only management accounting services, it is important that you find key partners to cover those things you do not.

It is vital that you do proper due diligence on any one you introduce to your clients. Remember your client's view of your business will be directly affected by their relationship with anyone you recommend.

As a reminder our key partners are:

- tax and compliance accountants (if you are not absolutely competent to do yourself)
- bookkeepers
- VAT experts
- payroll and pension service providers
- finance providers and brokers
- software systems providers
- HR advisors

If you don't know anyone in each of the service areas above, you can start off by asking other professionals you meet networking whom they would recommend - ideally because they have first-hand experience of working with the person they are recommending.

Becoming a one stop shop is a great way of adding value to your clients. One of mine likened me to the Yellow

Pages because I always knew someone who provided the particular business service he needed.

Tax and compliance accountants

I have found over the years that it is difficult to find tax and compliance accountants who will treat my clients as they should be treated.

Traditional high street accountants will often try to steal your clients if you are not careful, even though they are not able to offer our clients the services we can.

It is therefore important that you build a relationship with prospective accountants first, which allows you to properly vet whether you can trust them with your clients.

You may wish to recommend another CIMA MiP who does tax and compliance. If you do so, you should do the same due diligence on their aptitude to do the job required, and their suitability to work with your clients, as you would with any other key partner.

Of course it may be that a client already has a tax and compliance accountant they are happy with. In which case, you will need to build a good working relationship with these accountants so they don't undermine you.

Bookkeepers

A good bookkeeper is worth their weight in gold. They will do the processing work that needs to be done before we can start working our magic.

Some clients will have a bookkeeper on site already – either as an employee or as a subcontractor - but if a potential client does not have a bookkeeper you need to be able to recommend one you can work with.

Then you can either 'white label' the bookkeeping services within your own service offer, or the bookkeeper can work, and bill, independently under your supervision.

VAT Experts

VAT, as we know, was supposed to be the simple tax but has become more and more complex over the years.

Having a VAT expert you can call upon where your own knowledge and expertise is exhausted, can ensure your clients get the best help and advice.

Payroll and pension service providers

Payroll used to be a service any of us could offer our clients profitably. But in recent years it has been complicated by RTI and auto enrolment.

For this reason I would caution against offering payroll services yourself, not least because you will need to buy payroll software which links the HMRC and pension providers' systems. As we generally have only a small number of clients the need to purchase such software can make offering payroll ourselves uneconomic.

There are many payroll bureaus in the marketplace, that are better able to provide a cheap and effective service, and these bureaus often have relationships with pension providers.

As even the smallest companies will have to provide auto-enrolment pensions by the end of 2017 it is vital your clients have the best advice on what pension they should offer.

Finance providers and brokers

I have never worked for a client that has avoided using any form of external finance, so it is very important that you are aware of the finance providers and brokers who can assist your clients in finding the funding they need.

In particular you will need to develop good working relationships with the following:

- Banks
- Invoice financing providers
- Asset financing brokers
- Commercial mortgage providers
- Equity finance brokers

Funding providers can be good sources of leads and introductions so it is doubly important to find ones you can work with.

Software systems providers

All clients will need to have a financial software package to run their basic accounts.

There are many packages on the market but most clients will use Sage, Xero, or Quickbooks. It is very important

Kashflow

that you are familiar with how the reporting function works on any software package your client uses – and how to get the best out of it.

Becoming an expert in a particular software package can also offer a great opportunity to add value to clients as you can offer set up, training and optimisation services.

HR advisors and employment lawyers

Employers have a minefield of legislation to tackle and many will find themselves overwhelmed.

Having a good HR advisor at hand can help clients keep up to date on best practice and ensure they have the documentation available so they are compliant with employment law.

HR advisors and employment lawyers can also help clients out when faced with employee disputes.

EXERCISE

Create a list of those professionals you know already and would trust to serve your customers well. These are people you need to get to know better so organise to have a catch up with them over coffee.

If you don't have at least one professional in each of the sections I have highlighted make a note of any gaps and ensure you look out for professionals to fill those gaps when you are out networking.

Learning and action steps

Don't forget to fill this section – it can make a real difference to how much you learn from the handbook and how useful it is in helping you build the business you want.

Actions I will start doing   Importance   Date

Actions I will stop doing   Importance   Date

Behaviour change log

Today's date _____

Review Date	Reviewed	Outstanding Issues
Tomorrow		
1 week		
1 month		
3 months		

SECTION 5

FIXED PRICING

Show the way with fixed pricing

The old fashioned approach to pricing

Many accountants and other business professionals will charge an hourly rate. This safeguards the professional from under estimating the size of the job they are doing for their client; cushions against inefficient working; and makes it easier for them to quote a 'price'. However, it does nothing to foster good relationships between the professional and their clients.

Often the client has no idea the scale of the work being done for them and so has no idea of the size of likely bill. When the bill comes they may be completely unprepared for its size, suspect they are being over charged and question it.

The professional then has two options - stick to their guns and hope to make the client see the value of all the work they have done or reduce the size of the bill so the customer will pay. The first strategy may well end up with them losing the client: the second will only re-enforce the client's opinion that they were being over charged in the first place, leading both parties being unhappy with the compromise.

Bad practice case study - An accountant who treated their clients like mugs

I once had a client who had a compliance and tax accountant who charged by the hour. I could see no reason why they should not be able to fix a price for their work each year, as they knew the client and the amount of work required each year. I advised the client to ask them for a fixed fee so my client knew where they stood.

The accountant replied that they never worked for fixed fees, because in their experience once the fixed fee had been 'used up' work stopped, even if the end of the year had not been completed.

They preferred not to fix a fee because they could then charge clients fully for all the hours they had worked – even if it was their fault that the work was not done efficiently.

I was amazed. I asked my client what she would do if I just stopped working. "I'd walk away" she quite rightly replied.

Incidentally the client 'walked away' from their old accountant because she felt she was being treated like a mug. She went with one who could give a fixed price for a fixed scope of work.

Setting a fixed fee is not about setting a sum up to which you work. It is about having a clear agreement about how much the client will be charged for the job at hand - even if it does take a little longer than you thought.

There is a better way

As management accountants we have a duty to lead by example when it comes to financial dealings with our clients. After all how can we convince clients that we can help them with their pricing and debt collection strategies if our own are not ideal?

This is where fixed pricing comes in.

Having clear terms of businesses that state exactly what the package of work is, how much the client will be asked to pay - and when - is simply best practice. Better to agree what is expected from both parties before the work is undertaken, than to have to deal with misunderstandings afterwards.

The benefits of fixed pricing

➔ Everyone is on the same page and clients do not get any nasty surprises.

➔ You can set a monthly retainer with the client paying by standing order. This flattens out your income throughout the year irrespective of when you actually do the work and the client has a fixed flat fee every month.

➔ The particular benefit of setting up standing order retainers is that you are paid as an 'unavoidable' expense, rather than one the client has to consider when to pay. This is especially important where the client is experiencing cash flow problems and your inside knowledge means you may be reluctant to press for payment. There is no reason why you should finance your clients or be paid behind other suppliers.

→ By agreeing a fixed the client is agreeing to the scope and price of the work. If they initially think the job is too expensive you can look at ways to reduce the price by re-scoping or re-prioritising – but never by discounting!

If they still think you are too expensive you can walk away. Better to find out before you do the work that they cannot afford you, than afterwards when you are left out of pocket.

→ Because you are pricing the job, and not charging by the hour, you have the ability to optimise your price depending upon the situation of the customer and the importance of the project to their company.

→ But most importantly you are the professional and you should bear the risk of not pricing correctly - NOT THE CUSTOMER.

Fixed pricing for larger jobs

Now you may rightly argue that it can be difficult to fix a price for work (particularly with new clients) if the work is complex and/or of indeterminate scope. You would be right, but only because you would be trying to fix a price too early.

Where you are not clear what the scope of the work is, agree with the client that you will do a 'review' piece of work for a much smaller fixed fee. The review will clarify what is needed, and why, and once it is completed you will be much more confident in setting a fixed fee for the main piece of work.

Remember that where there are various defined stages to a large project it is best to set fixed fees only at the beginning of each stage. This will enable you to build in any changes in your knowledge of the customers' needs into your fixed pricing as you go from one stage to the next.

> Another bad practice case study - when is a fixed fee not a fixed fee?
>
> Another of my clients was paying an exorbitant amount to their accountant for basic compliance and tax work for his company and his family.
>
> Not only was he paying way over the odds, but his accountant was charging him for extras under the radar. My client was paying a fixed amount by standing order so he assumed that he was up to date with his bills. It turned out he wasn't. He still owed his old accountant a further £6,000, because the accountant regularly billed over the standing order amount – without expressly telling my client he was doing so.
>
> My client was pretty angry and set about telling his numerous business contacts about the sly tactics of an accountant he had previously thought highly of.

A fixed fee should always be a fixed fee. If you have got it wrong just put it down to experience and make sure you learn from your mistake. See the odd instance of over delivery as part of your marketing budget.

EXERCISE

If you do not already use fixed pricing for your clients go through each of them in turn and scope out the work you do for them each year. Then set a fixed fee for each of the services based on your knowledge of the customer's requirements.

At the end of the exercise add up the total for all the services and see how different it is from what you have charged them in the past. If there is very little difference I would switch to fixed fee pricing immediately.

If the fixed price is higher than customers are currently paying create a plan to show why the new fixed price appropriate. You will then be armed to negotiate the rise the next time you have a review with your clients and agree the services you will offer in the coming year.

Incidentally I would have service reviews with clients annually giving them the opportunity to voice any concerns and to value your role for the year ahead.

Learning and action steps

Don't forget to fill this section – it can make a real difference to how much you learn from the handbook and how useful it is in helping you build the business you want.

Actions I will start doing   Importance   Date

review pricing
- cash
- stapler
- care
follow up cust not won
- one call

Actions I will stop doing   Importance   Date

Behaviour change log

Today's date _____

Review Date	Reviewed	Outstanding Issues
Tomorrow		
1 week		
1 month		
3 months		

SECTION 6

Slowly, slowly catchy monkey

The problem with establishing our value

As I said earlier the concept of management accounting is not one that SME owners generally understand. Unfortunately no business owner is going to wake up in a cold sweat because they do not have a set of monthly management accounts!

If they have not had access to reliable, accurate and timely management information, they will not know the difference it can make to the control they have over their business finances, and their ability to make robust decisions. And if they don't know this they won't value what 'management accountants' can deliver. This means that we need to find ways to start opening their eyes to our value.

Bear in mind that it takes a greater degree of trust to invite someone like us into a business (i.e. someone who gets under the bonnet of their business and challenges them), than someone who is going to be on hand once a year to do statutory accounts and tax returns.

The business owner will need to be prepared to open up about what their financial concerns are.

MiPs will often get too excited about all the stuff they could do for a prospective client, but presenting a sweet shop full of solutions to all the problems they have will only scare them off. They won't understand half of the problems you see; they don't yet trust you enough to acknowledge they need your help; and so any costs you present them with (however, well thought though and fair in your eyes) will be unacceptable to them.

So, find the problem that is keeping your prospect up at night and start there. Offer a fixed price for sorting that particular problem out, do it well and on time, and it may well be that other work starts to flow from there.

Catching our monkey

Below are some areas you could offer assistance to build trust and provide quick value:

Cash Flow

Many business owners have trouble with their cash flow. They often don't understand why their cash flow is different from their profits and so there are key areas we can help them with.

➔ Debt collection

You will find that clients whose customers pay very slowly do so because the client does not have robust procedures for collecting what is owed to them.

They do not have firm terms of credit laid out in advance for customers; they do not invoice promptly after work has been completed; and once customers have been invoiced they do not have debt collection policies to ensure payments are made to agreed terms.

As management accountants we help business owners to correct all of these deficiencies and turn negative cash flow into a positive bank balance.

Whilst you may not think this is what you should be doing as a CIMA MiP, providing clear debt collection procedures is an effective method of helping business owners to understand how we can add value to their businesses.

You have an opportunity to do a small fixed fee piece of work to solve a real problem for the business owner and actually help them afford further work.

→ Financing — find contacts

SME owners often do not know where to look to find sources of finance. Very few will look further than their bank for funding options – which means they pay more interest than they need to, or may be turned down for funding they could get elsewhere.

Further, they will use inappropriate forms of financing. For example they may use overdraft financing for long term funding needs.

Of course, the situation is not helped by some banks that are quick to offer customers funding solutions such as invoice financing, even if they not the right source of funding for their customer's type of business - rather than more appropriate sources such as asset financing or EFG loans.

By having contacts in a variety funding providers you can facilitate more appropriate financing solutions for clients. As a bonus this can often lead to business planning work because, as we know, most funding providers will want clearly presented financial projections to help them assess a client's ability to pay.

The 'bank' of local finance providers you can call on to help your clients should include:

- A range of banks from high street providers to smaller customer focused banks such as Handelsbanken.

- Asset finance

- Invoice discounting (including those providing more tailored solutions)

- Brokers who can source a range of equity and loan finance solutions

- Commercial property finance

➔ Supplier management

I have met business owners who feel they should always pay suppliers very quickly. Whilst it is important that they keep good relationships with their suppliers many pay more quickly than their suppliers' credit terms - often because they don't know what these credit terms are.

Again this is where we can help establish good procedures.

Business planning

As mentioned earlier business planning is a key weapon in the arsenal of services we can offer.

I am so committed to business planning that I actually use it as a tool for assessing if a client is 'good' for me. After all if a business owner does not believe that having a well thought through and robust business plan is key to their business success, how are they going to value regular management information?

As we know business plans and forecasts provide context against which to measure results. If there is no plan how do we know if the business has delivered against the business owners own needs and expectations?

So, if a potential client does not have a business plan nor see the need in having one, I will not take them on as a retainer client. This avoids the scenario where my efforts are not valued and I just become a cost in the client's eyes.

The process of business planning also enables me to properly understand a client's business and the services they may need from me. Once we have done the planning together we can decide if we are right for each other.

If all goes well I have the information I need to come up with a fair fixed price for my services going forward. But if we decide to part ways, the client has a document they can use to move their business forward with another professional, or on their own.

But business planning can be more than a tool for assessing potential management accounting clients, or as a regular part of the service offered to these clients. Business planning can be a service in its own right for clients who may never want more regular work.

Business Planning Scenarios

One off business planning and forecasting can be a really nice filler. I have done business plans for potential business owners who want to model a new business idea, or to help evaluate a business they are hoping to buy. I have helped businesses with their funding applications by modelling their business in a way understood by the funding providers. I have also helped management teams assess whether a management buyout would work for them, given the business owner's perception of the value of the company.

All these have been valuable one- off pieces of work both in monetary terms and because they have given me new insights into different businesses.

Pricing

Effective pricing is a real problem for SMEs.

Many SMEs do not have the first idea how much their products or services cost them to produce. They will understand the 'easy to see' costs, but fail to take into account business running costs, when they decide how much to charge. Some do not even have the confidence to charge a fair price and persuade themselves they have to undercut the competition - even if that competition is not providing the same level of service or quality of product.

As with so many things in business it all comes down to confidence - in terms of their own products or services and in terms of their place in the market.

Here we can help enormously. By properly assessing their cost base we can help business owners to understand the minimum they should be charging and we can help them look for cost savings if this minimum is too high. We can help them to understand the true value of their offering so they are more confident in charging the appropriate rate.

Sometimes business owners base their pricing on entirely the wrong aspect of the service they provide - often because this wrong aspect is easiest to understand.

Pricing Case Study

A client of mine who ran a virtual phone answering service used to price by adding £1 per call to the cost of that call. This meant that a lawyer would be paying far less per month than a plumber as he received fewer calls. The fact that each call was worth far more in sales to the lawyer than the plumber was irrelevant in this model.

We set up a new model of fixed monthly pricing for each client. My client came to understand that the value for her customers was not the couple of minutes of call time, but the fact that knowledgeable and professional staff were at the end of the phone representing them.

Our objective viewpoint can help our clients see what *their* customers value in their service, so they can price effectively and earn the revenues they deserve.

You can offer a pricing review as a one off piece of work, for a fixed fee, which will add real value to business of all sizes.

These are just some of the one off services you could think about providing - be imaginative and think of ways you can provide a small service at no great cost to help potential clients understand the value you could bring.

EXERCISE

Think about the broad area of management accountancy work and list those tasks you could do for an SME to unstick particular problems.

bookkeeping

credit control / debt collection
- *ensure credit terms understood*
- *by cust*
- *enforce credit terms*
- *chase - clear step procedure*

pricing

accounts & budgets

Learning and action steps

Don't forget to fill this section - it can make a real difference to how much you learn from the handbook and how useful it is in helping you build the business you want.

Actions I will start doing	Importance	Date

Actions I will stop doing	Importance	Date

Behaviour change log

Today's date _____

Review Date   Reviewed   Outstanding Issues

Tomorrow

1 week

1 month

3 months

SECTION 7

Strategic Introducers

Our sales team

We have already discussed the fact that most SMEs do not know what a management accountant/part time FD does, or how we can support their business.

However, there are people out there who do understand, and I call them strategic introducers. They can become part of our sales team if we harness them effectively.

Strategic introducers

Strategic introducers are those professionals who offer non-competing services to your ideal client base. Often these professionals, like us, have worked in large corporations at managerial level and so have had first-hand experience of the benefits of sound financial information.

They also know their clients and where deficiencies in their finance 'department' may be - these deficiencies may even adversely affect the strategic introducer's ability to do their job well.

Over the years I have found that the best strategic introducers come from the following sources:

- Sales and marketing professionals
- Business coaches
- Funding brokers - particularly where there is a management buyout or where their clients need proper business plans to enable them to get the funding required

- IFAs - if they are owner/managers of a company with multiple advisors
- IT companies and website developers

There are a couple of omissions you may find surprising - namely other accountants, lawyers and banks.

Other accountants tend to be poor referrers, even if they only concentrate on tax and compliance - maybe because they worry they should be providing the services we do, but cannot. Lawyers just don't understand referrals to other professionals at all, unless the referrals are to other professionals in the legal world.

Banks, on the other hand, are reluctant to refer specific individuals in case they are accused of inappropriate favoritism - however, I have had several great referrals of other strategic introducers from banks like Handelsbanken.

Useless for more expensive

Finding strategic introducers

The owners/managers of the types of businesses that would make good clients for us, do not tend to go networking – with the possible exception of IOD events.

However, for our target strategic introducers networking is a key way of getting to meet *their* strategic introducers. So it is important that you choose your networking carefully to give yourself the best opportunity of meeting the right professionals. Try several types of event on for size and concentrate on who is in the room, rather than the style of networking on offer.

Once you have identified someone of interest make sure you follow through and book a 121 over coffee to start the 'getting to know you' process.

Choosing strategic partners

Ideally with any business relationship there will be an element of quid pro quo. Strategic introducers are most likely to keep you in the front of their minds if you are keeping them at the front of yours.

But you should only refer another professional if you are confident about the quality of the services they offer. Just as you should vet your key partners, so you should vet your strategic introducers. Once you are happy with what they offer they can then become full strategic partners.

> Strategic partnership case study
>
> I have a very good strategic partner who is a marketing strategist. He was engaged by his client to get more customers.
>
> When he asked which their current most profitable customers were, the client was unable to say. When he asked which of their products or services were most profitable they were similarly unable to tell him.
>
> This lack of knowledge severely limited his ability to find the 'right' customers for them. So he said "You need Fiona". He introduced me into the business and we have been working together ever since.

EXERCISE

Create a list of the professionals you know who you think might make great strategic introducers for you or who you may be happy to introduce to your clients. You should be building relationships with all of them and meeting with them regularly.

Mark Biddlecombe

Learning and action steps

Don't forget to fill this section – it can make a real difference to how much you learn from the handbook and how useful it is in helping you build the business you want.

Actions I will start doing   <u>Importance</u>   <u>Date</u>

Actions I will stop doing   <u>Importance</u>   Date

Behaviour change log

Today's date _____

Review Date	Reviewed	Outstanding Issues
Tomorrow		
1 week		
1 month		
3 months		

SECTION 8

Your marketing and sales plan

Getting some help

We are accountants, not marketing or sales managers. For this reason I think it is important to seek help when deciding what your marketing and sales plan should look like. How you will reach your target audience, and how you can build trust with potential clients, is likely to be far easier for you to determine with professional guidance than if you try to struggle through on your own.

Just as we would not expect business owners to be able to do their financial strategy without our help, why should we expect to be able do our own marketing and sales strategy without some help?

One way of getting great value marketing/sales strategy work for your business could be to offer a quid pro quo with the professional you are keen to work with. In exchange for them doing your marketing/sales strategy you could do forecasting work for their business.

The added benefit to both of you of this approach is that, at the end of the process you will each have a good idea of how the other works and this will make it easier for you to recommend one another other.

As well as good strategy it is important to make sure that your marketing collateral is professionally designed and printed (where appropriate).

If you are having a website built make sure that it is professionally designed, and optimised, to give you the best possibility of reaching those you are aiming to impress.

Even though there are packages and apps out there, which will allow you to do it yourself, do not fall into the trap of thinking this is the best way forward. Some of the worst websites I have come across have been put together using off the shelf apps by people who don't really know what they are doing.

You will be working for professionals who are expecting a professional service from you. You will not be able to encourage them to see your professionalism if your website is poor.

Nuggets I have learned

Although you will need professional sales and marketing guidance there are specific things I can share about marketing my own business:

→ Networking

As we know networking is a great way to meet other business people.

In my opinion it is the best way for meeting both strategic introducers and key partners for your business.

When you are networking remember you are your business's best and only asset. Ensure that you are dressed for the occasion in a professional way and be prepared to follow up on leads in a similarly professional way.

→ Business Cards

I have a drawer full of business cards from people I simply cannot remember. I am hopeless with names but great with faces – the trouble is that very few business cards have photos on. Also very few business cards have any details about what the person actually does.

After a while I have a cull because there is no way I will be contacting any of these individuals - I simply cannot remember why I should!

If you are going to go to the trouble of having business cards printed, produce something people can refer to at a later date once they are back in their offices.

Below is a copy of the folded A5 business card I give out to give you some tips on what you may like to do.

Front Page

Mastering your business finances is the key to having a successful business

Ensure lack of financial knowledge and understanding doesn't hold your business back

Middle Section

"Fiona... has an incredible ability to collate, simplify and explain financial data that can then be understood and used by any non-finance manager, all delivered with patience, courtesy and, most importantly round here, a sense of humour."
John Dalton

Relevant Information for Your Business... Today

Many businesses grow rapidly in the early years but their management reporting and financial systems often lag behind.

This means that business owners and managers often make decisions without all the information they need to achieve the best outcomes.

I can do a thorough review of your financial systems and processes to help your staff deliver the best, and most relevant, information for your business today. If there is a gap at the top of your finance department I also offer virtual FD services.

Customer, Product and Project Profitability

Successful businesses understand where profit is derived. This is not as simple as running a profit and loss account every month, but requires analysis of the detail behind the headlines.

In particular, it is important to understand, which customers, products and projects bring profit into the business. Such knowledge can mean future sales and marketing effort is targeted to maximise future profit.

I set up systems to provide this information regularly.

Financial Training

Entrepreneurs, and non-financial managers, have a specific way of looking at the world which means they can see opportunities others can't.

However, they often lack the knowledge needed to understand the financial aspects of their business.

I can run Finance for Non-financial Managers courses, tailored specifically for your business, so that anyone who requires it can get the financial grounding they need.

I also do specific Sage and general technical training for your finance staff. This can be on a one to one or group basis.

Business and Financial Planning

Having a well thought through budget can help a business measure progress towards its financial targets. If there are problems they can be identified so action can be taken at the earliest point.

I help businesses to build relevant plans and budgets – along with the reporting systems to measure progress against them – so they are best equipped to monitor their success.

"She has really helped me look at my budget, P&L and general spend and we work very closely together getting the months and years ahead planned! Fiona also provides great support for my Finance Manager." Helen Lacey

Back Page

I am a business person just like you.

My background is in management accounting. This means my focus is on providing business people with current financial information, which will help them make the right decisions for them.

I also help with planning for the future so businesses are more likely to reach their goals.

I have worked with, and for, a wide range of different businesses in an extensive range of business areas.

PRACTISING CERTIFICATE HOLDER

I am a Chartered Management Accountant and have nearly 25 years experience working in business. This means you can rest assured that YOUR business is in safe hands.

Contact Me:

Fiona Bevan

➜ Newsletters

Producing a newsletter can be a very good way of reminding clients, prospects and strategic partners of what we do and, in some cases where we haven't seen them for a while, that we still exist.

If you are going down this route think about making your newsletter as user friendly as possible with reference to other businesses and helpful tips and hints which will help a business owner master their finances.

Accountants often make the mistake of filling a newsletter with summaries of the recent budget or other information clients just find boring. As my friend Trevor would say 'I pay my accountant to know that stuff so I don't need to!'

Also think about producing hard copy newsletters for a smaller audience rather than emailing newsletters for everyone. I get huge numbers of email newsletters every month and generally just delete them, because I haven't time to read them all.

However, a hard copy newsletter sent through the post is something different. We get very little through the post these days, so your newsletter will stand out – especially if it is in a bright envelope. A printed newsletter can also be read anywhere – even on the loo!

For inspiration copies of my newsletters can be found on my website fionabevanfinancialmanagement.co.uk and clicking on the link on the home page or by going to: *https://brightbusinessbulletin.wordpress.com*

➔ LinkedIn

I have found LinkedIn to be a great way of getting myself known in the marketplace. Ensuring your profile is up to date, and asking for recommendations, can help people find you online.

You can also write articles/blogs to demonstrate your skills and knowledge, which will help prospects understand what you do, even if you don't have a website.

EXERCISE

Think very carefully about exactly the types of clients you wish to attract and write down their characteristics. This will help your sales/marketing professional create a strategy to get the clients you need.

But you can start by getting your LinkedIn profile up to date and asking for recommendations from those you have worked for previously – even recommendations for work you did as an employee is relevant if you did management accounting work.

Learning and action steps

Don't forget to fill this section – it can make a real difference to how much you learn from the handbook and how useful it is in helping you build the business you want.

Actions I will start doing   <u>Importance</u>   <u>Date</u>

regularly request recommendations

Actions I will stop doing   <u>Importance</u>   Date

Behaviour change log

Today's date _____

Review Date	Reviewed	Outstanding Issues
Tomorrow		
1 week		
1 month		
3 months		

SECTION 9

Summary - reaching your pot of gold

You are most likely to build the business you want if you know what your ideal business looks like.

If you have clear goals in terms of take home income, the work you want to do and the types of clients you want to work for, you will have a much improved chance of getting there.

Don't be afraid to niche – in fact you will greatly increase your ability to sell your message in the market place if you do.

Concentrate on what you are very good at and don't worry about providing services you are not experienced or learned enough to offer. Instead find other professionals to provide these services to your clients on your behalf.

Make sure you have good processes and procedures in place in your own business. After all your business is no different from any other – good practice is good practice whatever size a business is, or whatever sector they are in.

If clients are to believe that you are the right person to invite into their business it is vital for you to be congruent with the message you are sending out.

For example, if you are a big exponent of business planning you should have a full business plan for your business (and not just the numbers bit!).

If you are looking to help businesses optimise their cash flow you should have robust procedures in your business for: setting out terms of business; invoicing promptly; and then have debt collection procedures in line with your terms of business.

It is important that we lead by example.

Don't try to sell the sweet shop to new clients, unless they have a clear understanding that what they need is a FD type person.

Start with smaller pieces of work that allow you to demonstrate your value. Once you have earned your client's trust it will be easier to move onto providing more regular services.

Finding the right retainer clients will take time but once you have found them they will be very reluctant to let you go.

Finally, we are professionals. We should value other professionals – or how can we hope that they will value us? Use other professionals where your business requires it and don't try to do it all yourself.

After all we know that business owners often get themselves into financial difficulty because they try to do everything themselves.

A final note from Fiona

This handbook is not designed to be read just once and then put on a bookshelf to gather dust. Please do revisit your action and behaviour change logs at the end of each section, to track how your learning is helping move your business forward.

I hope you have found this handbook useful – if so please tell other Mips you know.

If you haven't found it useful because you have not understood it all, please let me know so I can make changes to future additions.

You can also contact me if you require 121 mentoring.

You can contact me at:
fiona@fionabevanfinancialmanagement.co.uk

22460856R00042

Printed in Great Britain
by Amazon